The Tattered Unicorn

The Tattered Unicorn

by
NM Reed
&
McCarthy Preston

Story by NMReed
Artwork by NM Reed and AI software: Davinci
c 2024
NMReedBooks.com

To order additional copy of this book, contact:
NMReedBooks.com
and TatteredUnicronPublishing.com

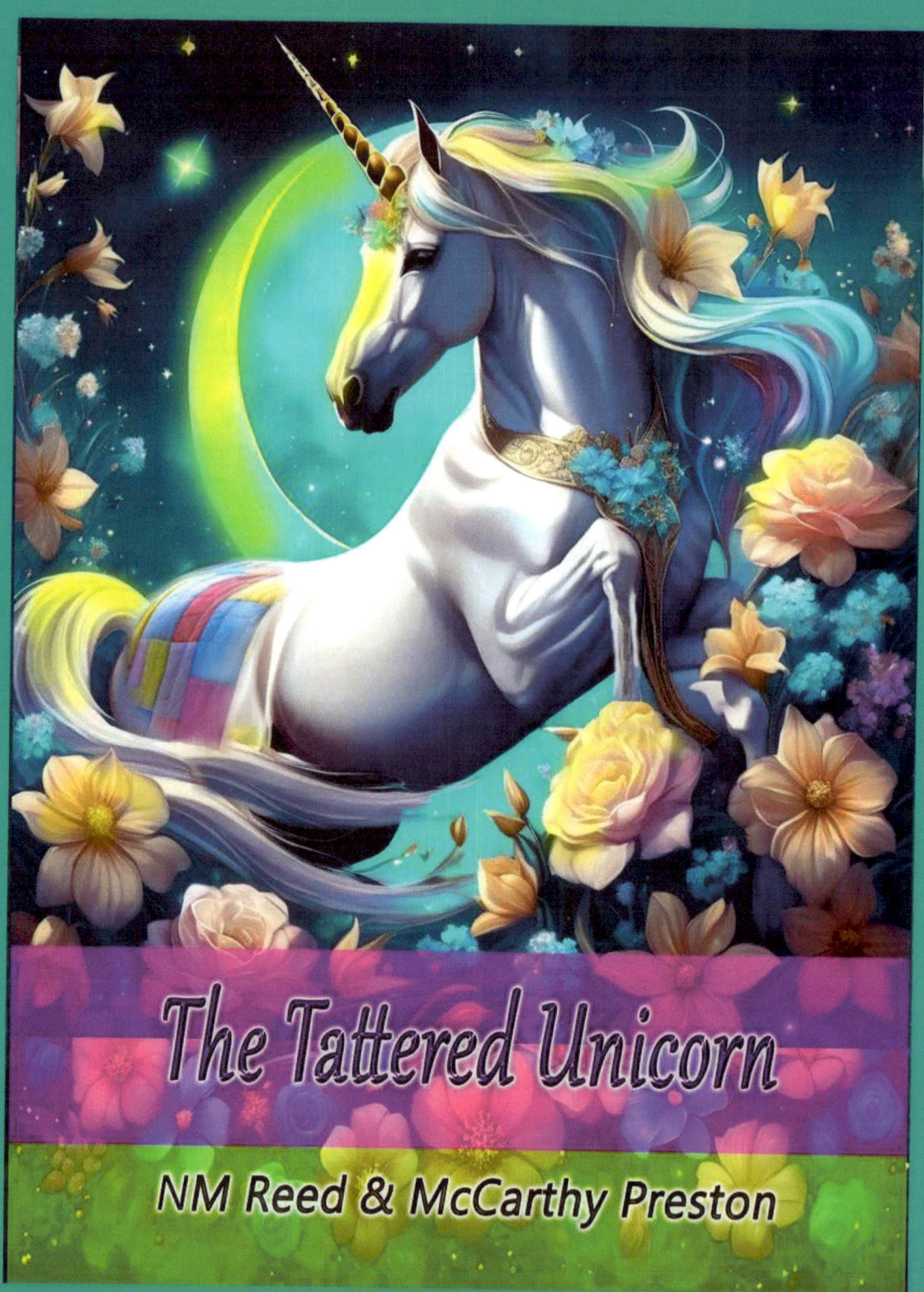

The Tattered Unicorn

NM Reed & McCarthy Preston

The Tattered Unicorn

NM Reed & McCarthy Preston

The Tattered Unicorn

A unicorn named Frost lived in the forest with his friends. He got curious one day and followed down the path toward the city. There he saw sights unknown. He met a God and Goddess who loved him, but they asked too much of him. When he tried to go home, they attacked. How does Frost get home? What happens on his homeward journey, and who helps heal his wounds?
40 pages of beautiful AI rendered unicorn artwork by NM Reed and Davinci

NMReedBooks.com

Frost the Unicorn lived in the forest with his friends.

By day they played in the sun and flowers.

And they slept under the trees by night.

Frost and his friends were proud to be unicorns.

Frost looked down the valley and saw the city. "How beautiful."

One day he decided to go look, down the path toward the city to see.

Shining cities like crystals he did not understand.

He arrived in the city with crystal towers all around.
People walked by and by and no one noticed him.

He looked between the tall buildings from the dark alleybelow,
"What is going on here?" And no one heard.

Then a deep voice spoke from above, "This is my city, meek one.
Where wonders abound and dreams come true."

"That sounds good," said Frost, unsure.
"Most people think so," said Mowra, the architect of all.

My, aren't you beautiful," said Vanity, Mowra's wife.
"But, we'll have to do something about all that hair."

"But, where do I sleep?" asked Frost.
"There's no green grass to sleep on or trees to sleep under?"

"You'll get those things when you get a job," said Vanity.
"And that golden horn! Don't you someday want to become a real
horse?".

The beautiful unicorn lost its rainbow colors and was starting to turn gray.
So he turned to run for home, to the forests, fields and his friends.

"You cant just leave!" cried Vanity.
"You must stay and learn!" cried Mowra.
But Frost held his impressive head up, and
turned and bolted out of town.

16

"You will worship me!" screamed Vanity.
And the unicorn ran clattering down the street out of town.

"What are these mean black birds?"
thought Frost as they chased him out of the city.

Vanity's mocking birds chased the unicorn on into the night.
The birds tore holes in his beautiful white hide. He ran and ran.
And still he could not shake them off

Frost ran through the night. And the birds fought him, crying,
"Worship Me! Worship Me!" Vanity's shrill voice loud in his ears.

Finally the birds flew away and left the unicorn alone.
Frost stood still, breathing frozen crystals in the air.

Frost wandered alone and afraid in a part of the forest he did not know.
But he knew the emerging starlight lit his path toward home.

Frost the Unicorn was sore and tired.
But he conjured his best magic and persevered.

Finally Vanity's mocking birds left him alone. He lay in the
cool grass with the flowers shining in the moonlight.

As Frost lay down to rest, the morning sky goddess Aurora appeared above him. "My sweetness, you have suffered. Lay still and be healed."

"What are you going to do to me?" cried Frost, afraid.
"I can fix this, if you just hold still," said Aurora softly.
"You are a Tattered Unicorn."

Come, My Beauty. You are tattered all over," Aurora crooned.
And Aurora and his friends sewed his wounds with bits of morning
sky into a blanket of patchworks.

Aurora sewed and worked, pinching and tickling Frost's torn white hide. The pain soon stopped and Frost felt much better, thanks to the Goddess and his friends.

Aurora looked at his new patchwork rump.
"There now, good as new. Wear your scars with pride, Frost."

And although his fur was altered,
he felt happy and was glad to be with friends.

He grew proud of his patchwork fur. And once again he could
dance in starlight and twirl in moonbeams.

Frost felt complete again living in the trees with Aurora's patchwork of morning sky lights on his rump.

More books by the authors

NM Reed & McCarthy Preston

The Littlest Coyote series
of children's books
The Worrisome War of the Whimsical Wizards The
Dueling Wizards of Simpletown

available at
NMReedBooks.com
Walmart.com
BarnesandNoble.com
Amazon.com
GooglePlay

=

Thank you!!
More illustrated stories to come.
From NMReedBooks.com
and TatteredUnicronPublishing.com